Poems to make your Friends Laugh

chosen by Susie Gibbs

illustrated by
Jess Mikhail

OXFORD
UNIVERSITY PRESS

OXFORD
UNIVERSITY PRESS

Great Clarendon Street, Oxford OX2 6DP

Oxford University Press is a department of the University of Oxford.
It furthers the University's objective of excellence in research, scholarship,
and education by publishing worldwide in
Oxford New York
Auckland Bangkok Buenos Aires Cape Town Chennai
Dar es Salaam Delhi Hong Kong Istanbul Karachi Kolkata
Kuala Lumpur Madrid Melbourne Mexico City Mumbai Nairobi
São Paulo Shanghai Taipei Tokyo Toronto

This selection and arrangement copyright © Susie Gibbs 2003

Illustrations by Jess Mikhail 2003
Designed by You Know Who

The moral rights of the author have been asserted

Database right Oxford University Press (maker)

First published 2003

British Library Cataloguing in Publication Data available

ISBN 0-19-276291 5

3 5 7 9 10 8 6 4 2

Typeset by Mary Tudge (Typesetting Services)

Printed in Great Britain
by Cox & Wyman Ltd, Reading, Berkshire

Contents

Could Have Been Worse

My friends have not seen London,
They've never been to France,
But yesterday at recess
They saw my underpants.

I kicked a ball, my skirt flew up
And I know what they saw.
The girls all stared and blushed and laughed,
The boys said, 'Oo-la-la!'

I've thought a lot about it.
This conclusion I have drawn:
I'm embarrassed that they saw them,
But I'm glad I had them on.

Bill Dodds

Remember Me?

What will they say
When I've gone away:
He was handsome? He was fun?
He shared his gum? He wasn't
Too dumb or too smart? He
Played a good game of volley ball?
Or will they only say
He stepped in the dog doo
At Jimmy Altman's party?

Judith Viorst

Bare Back Riding

I've ridden a New Forest pony,
I've ridden a camel too;
I've ridden a wonky donkey,
And a llama in darkest Peru;
I've ridden a mule in Morocco,
But there's one thing I don't recommend:
That's riding a hedgehog naked,
Cos it don't half hurt your rear end.

Mike Jubb

Comicosaurus

Here's a jolly dinosaur,
he likes to tickle you,
and tickle, tickle, tickle till
your face turns red and blue.

His laugh is loud and merry,
even if his breath smells bad,
but he keeps it up for hours and hours
and drives you deaf and mad.

Then he pulls your leg a bit
(he likes his little joke)
and snaps it off above the knee
and shoves it down his throat.

So even though it laughs a lot
and has a charming smile,
you'd be mad as a hatter
to stop to chatter
with a massive flesh-eating reptile.

Dave Calder

There was a young Lady of Spain

There was a young lady of Spain,
Who was dreadfully sick in the train,
    And again and again and again and again,
And again and again and again.

Anon.

There was a young Lady of Wilts

There was a young lady of Wilts
Who walked all through Scotland on stilts;
When they said, 'Oh how shocking
To show so much stocking!'
She said, 'How about you and your kilts?'

Anon.

There was a young Lady of Malta

There was a young lady of Malta
Who strangled her aunt with a halter.
She said, 'I won't bury her,
She'll do for my terrier;
She'll keep for a month if I salt her.'

Anon.

The Flipper-Flopper Bird

O have you never ever heard
Of the Flipper-Flopper Bird?
O have you never seen his teeth,
Two above and one beneath?

O have you never known the thrill
Of stroking his enormous bill?
O have you never taken tea
With him sitting up a tree?

O have you never seen him hop
As he goes a-flip, a-flop?
O have you never heard his cry?
No, you've never? Nor have I.

Colin West

Miss Muffet

Little Miss Muffet
Sat on a tuffet
Eating some Irish stew.
Down came a spider
That sat down beside her
And so she ate him, too.

Anon.

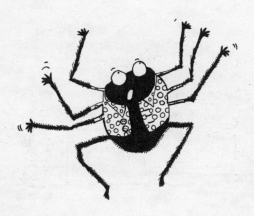

Your Face and Mine

Roses are red
Cabbages are green
My face may be funny
But yours is a scream.

Anon.

Some People Say that Fleas Are Black

Some people say that fleas are black,
But I know it isn't so;
For Mary had a little lamb
Whose fleas was white as snow.

Anon.

Doctor Bell

Doctor Bell fell down the well
And broke his collarbone.
Doctors should attend the sick
And leave the well alone.

Anon.

Ode To My Nose

O Nose
Why perch upon my Face?
Could you not find
A better place?

You jut between
One Eye and t'other
So neither Eye
Can see his Brother.

An easy target
For the hostile Fist.
You're an obstruction
When I want to be kissed.

And when you run
It's always South
Over my top lip
Into my Mouth.

O Nose
Why perch upon my Face?
Could you discover
No better place?

My Nose replied:
Up here I have come
As far as possible
From your Bum.

Adrian Mitchell

Kitty

Look at pretty little Kitty
Gnawing on a bone!
How I wish she'd eat some fish
And leave my leg alone.

Doug MacLeod

wheN you Get Old

When you get old
And think you're sweet
Pull off your shoes
And smell your feet.

Anon.

Fuzzy-wuzzy

Fuzzy-Wuzzy was a bear
Fuzzy-Wuzzy had no hair
So Fuzzy-Wuzzy wasn't fuzzy, wuzzy?

Anon.

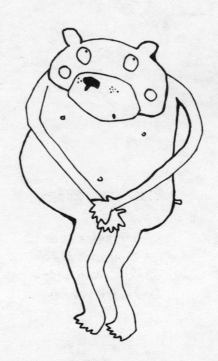

Algy Met a Bear

Algy met a bear,
A bear met Algy.
The bear was bulgy,
The bulge was Algy.

Anon.

Epitaph oN a 'maRf'

Wot a marf 'e'd got,
Wot a marf.
When 'e wos a kid,
Goo' Lor' luv'll
'Is pore old muvver
Must 'a' fed 'im wiv a shuvvle.

Wot a gap 'e'd got,
Pore chap,
'E'd never been known to larf,
Cos if 'e did
It's a penny to a quid
'E'd 'a' split 'is fice in 'arf.

Anon.

Two of a Kind

My foot and its toes, I suppose,
Are a bit like my nose, I suppose.
For as far as I can tell,
They both stick out and SMELL!

Ian Souter

Something's There

Something's there
In the Frigidaire—
Something long forgotten,
Something ruined and rotten.
Way in the back—
Green and black.
Behind the eggs—
I think it has legs.
Something stale—
Do I see a tail?
Check it out—
Is that a snout?

Let's go eat out.

Douglas Florian

Hello! How Are You? I Am Fine!

Hello! How are you? I am fine!
is all my dog will say,
he's probably repeated it
a thousand times today.
He doesn't bark his normal bark,
he doesn't even whine,
he only drones the same *Hello!*
How are you? I am fine!

Hello! How are you? I am fine!
his message doesn't change,
it's gotten quite monotonous,
and just a trifle strange.
Hello! How are you? I am fine!
it makes the neighbours stare,
they're unaware that yesterday
he ate my talking bear.

Jack Prelutsky

Oh, How Strange

Oh, how strange is my Uncle Ned!
He wears a cat on his balding head.
When asked why he wears a cat for a wig,
He says that he sneezes when wearing a pig.

Paul Duggan

The Cabbage is a Funny Veg

The cabbage is a funny veg.
All crisp, and green, and brainy.
I sometimes wear one on my head
When it's cold and rainy.

Roger McGough

Oh, Ozzie!

'Polar bear in the garden!' yelled Ozzie,
And we all rushed out to see,
But of course it wasn't a bear at all—
Just a marmalade cat who'd jumped over the wall.
Oh, Ozzie!

'Mountain lion in the garden!' yelled Ozzie,
And we all rushed out to see,
But of course it wasn't a lion with a roar—
Just the scruffy black dog who'd dug in from next door.
Oh, Ozzie!

'Kangaroo in the garden!' yelled Ozzie,
And we all stayed in and smiled,
And of course it wasn't a kangaroo—
But a man-eating tiger escaped from the zoo.
Poor Ozzie.

Richard Edwards

Down with Flu!

I've a bag code,
fluey and flemmy
in me node;

feel like somebobby's
stuffed
a hod wet towel
insibe
me achin' heb;

I've a scratchy frob
in me throbe,
me chest's full
ob frobspawn;

I wheeze and explose
ashoo-ashoo-ashoo
into me hankersneeze,
I tishoo-tishoo-tishoo
into me tishoo;

I've a bag code
in me node,
and I'm feb up,
really feb up,

really, really, really
feb up here in beb.

Matt Simpson

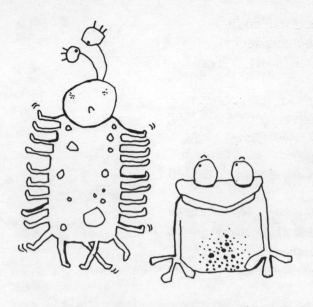

A Centipede

A centipede was happy quite
Until a frog in fun
Said, 'Pray, which leg comes after which?'
This raised her mind to such a pitch,
She lay distracted in a ditch,
Considering how to run.

Anon.

Old Mrs Thing-um-e-bob

Old Mrs Thing-um-e-bob,
  Lives at you-know-where,
Dropped her what-you-may-call-it down
  The well of the kitchen stair.

'Gracious me!' said Thing-um-e-bob,
  'This don't look too bright.
I'll ask old Mr What's-his-name
  To try and put it right.'

Along came Mr What's-his-name,
  He said, 'You've broke the lot!
I'll have to see what I can do
  With some of the you-know-what.'

So he gave the what-you-may-call-it a pit
  And he gave it a bit of a pat,
And he put it all together again
  With a little of this and that.

And he gave the what-you-may-call-it a dib
  And he gave it a dab as well
When all of a sudden he heard a note
  As clear as any bell.

'It's as good as new!' cried What's-his-name.
  'But please remember, now,
In future, Mrs Thing-um-e-bob
  You'll have to go you-know-how.'

Charles Causley

Lim

There once was a bard of Hong Kong
Who thought limericks were too long.

Gerard Benson

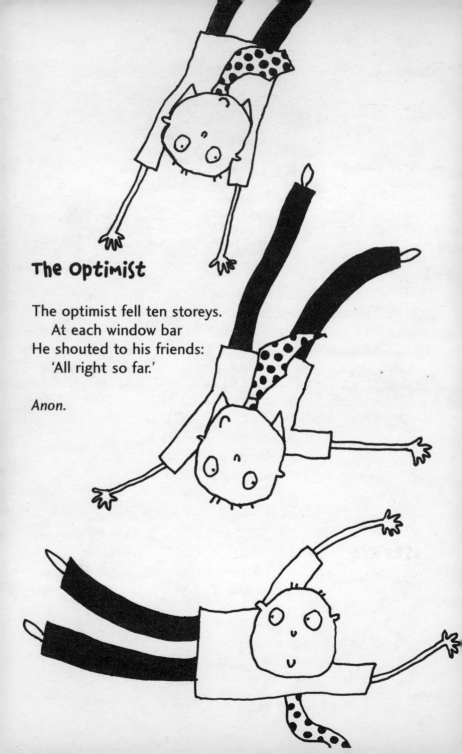

The Optimist

The optimist fell ten storeys.
   At each window bar
He shouted to his friends:
   'All right so far.'

Anon.

An Epicure Dining at Crewe

An epicure dining at Crewe
Once found a large mouse in his stew.
   Said the waiter, 'Don't shout
   And wave it about,
Or the rest will be wanting one, too!'

Anon.

Quick

Quick! Quick!
The cat's been sick.

Where? Where?
Under the chair.

Hasten! Hasten!
Fetch a basin.

Too late. Too late.
The carpet's in an awful state.

Alas! Alas! All in vain.
The cat has licked it up again.

Anon.

There Once was an Old Jellyfish

There once was an old jellyfish,
Who said, very sadly, 'I wish
I lived in the Red Sea,
For then I would be
A redcurrant jellyfish.'

Anon.

Appreciation

Auntie, did you feel no pain
Falling from that willow tree?
Will you do it, please, again?
'Cos my friend here didn't see.

Harry Graham

The Wizard Said:

'You find a sheltered spot that faces south . . .'
  'And then?'
'You sniff and put two fingers in your mouth . . .'
  'And then?'
'You close your eyes and roll your eyeballs round . . .'
  'And then?'
'You lift your left foot slowly off the ground . . .'
  'And then?'
'You make your palm into a kind of cup . . .'
  'And then?'
'You *very quickly* raise your right foot up . . .'
  'And then?'
'You fall over.'

Richard Edwards

The Thinker

There was a young fellow who thought
Very little, but thought it a lot.
   Then at long last he knew
   What he wanted to do,
But before he could start, he forgot.

John Ciardi

There was a young man from Bengal

There was a young man from Bengal
Who went to a fancy dress ball.
   He thought he would risk it
   And go as a biscuit,
But a dog ate him up in the hall.

Anon.

Do Not Spit

There was an old man of Darjeeling
Who travelled from London to Ealing.
It said on the door,
'Please don't spit on the floor',
So he carefully spat on the ceiling.

Anon.

Here is the Feather warcast

In the South it will be a dowdy clay
with some shattered scours.
Further North there'll be some hoe and snail
with whales to the guest.
In the East the roaring pain
will give way to some psalmy bun.

Trevor Millum

My Sister

My sister's remarkably light,
She can float to a fabulous height.
It's a troublesome thing,
But we tie her with string,
And we use her instead of a kite.

Margaret Mahy

Song Sung by a Man on a Barge to Another Man on a Different Barge in Order to Drive Him Mad

Oh,

I am the best bargee bar none,
You are the best bargee bar one!
You are the second-best bargee,
You are the best bargee bar me!

Oh,

I am the best . . .

(and so on, until he is
hurled into the canal)

Kit Wright

Runny Egg

For breakfast I had a runny egg.
I chased it round the table.
It wobbled and it screeched at me.
'Catch me if you're able!'

So I nailed it to the table.

Brian Patten

Cockroach Sandwich

Cockroach sandwich
For my lunch,
Hate the taste
But love the crunch!

Colin McNaughton

At My Birthday Party

At my birthday party
I had chocolate cake,
And cheesecake,
And fruitcake,
And ginger cake,
And fudge cake.
After that I had stummer cake.

Anthony Browne

zebra Question

I asked the zebra,
Are you black with white stripes?
Or white with black stripes?
And the zebra asked me,
Are you good with bad habits?
Or are you bad with good habits?
Are you noisy with quiet times?
Or are you quiet with noisy times?
Are you happy with some sad days?
Or are you sad with some happy days?
Are you neat with some sloppy ways?
Or are you sloppy with some neat ways?
And on and on and on and on
And on and on he went.
I'll never ask a zebra
About stripes
Again.

Shel Silverstein

The Sausage is a Cunning Bird

The sausage is a cunning bird
With feathers long and wavy—
It swims about in the frying pan
And lays its eggs in gravy.

Anon.

The Common Cormorant

The common cormorant or shag
Lays eggs inside a paper bag
The reason you will see no doubt
It is to keep the lightning out.
But what these unobservant birds
Have never noticed is that herds
Of wandering bears may come with buns
And steal the bags to hold the crumbs.

Christopher Isherwood

Under the Apple Tree

As I sat under the apple tree
A birdie sent his love to me
And as I wiped it from my eye
I said 'Thank goodness cows can't fly.'

Anon.

what Makes Me me

I've been told I've got
Mum's ears
Dad's hair
Gran's chin
Aunty Bee's sense of humour
And Grandpa Don's laugh.

Will they ever want them back, d'you think?

James Carter

Elephant Rules

Never be silly or mean
To an elephant,
Never feed chili or beans
To an elephant,
Never go near
To the front or the rear
Of a chiliful, bellyful
Smellyphant.

David L. Harrison

The Sleepy Giant

My age is three hundred and seventy-two,
    And I think, with the deepest regret,
How I used to pick up and voraciously chew
    The dear little boys whom I met.

I've eaten them raw, in their holiday suits;
    I've eaten them curried with rice;
I've eaten them baked, in their jackets and boots,
    And found them exceedingly nice.

But now that my jaws are weak for such fare,
    I think it exceedingly rude
To do such a thing, when I'm quite well aware
    Little boys do not like to be chewed.

And so I contentedly live upon eels,
    And try to do nothing amiss,
And I pass all the time I can spare from my meals
    In innocent slumber—like this.

C. E. Carryl

The Bug and the Flea

A bug and a flea
Went to sea
On a reel of cotton.

The bug was drowned
The flea was found
Stuck to a mermaid's bottom.

Anon.

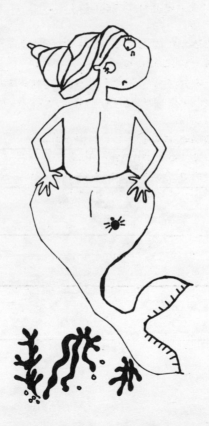

Toot! Toot!

A peanut sat on a railroad track,
His heart was all a-flutter;
The five-fifteen came rushing by—
Toot! Toot! Peanut butter!

Anon.

O, MOON!

O, Moon! when I look on your beautiful face
Careering along through the darkness of space,
The thought has frequently come to my mind,
If ever I'll gaze on your lovely behind.

Anon.

I'll Be Darned

Said the toe to the sock,
'Let me through, let me through!'

Said the sock to the toe,
'I'll be darned if I do.'

Anon.

Snap

Thanks for the photo
It really was nice
I put it in the attic
To scare away the mice.

Anon.

Dinosaur Department

Clever Clem went out of doors,
Playing with the dinosaurs,
Telling others in his class,
'Not to worry. They eat grass.'
A snap, a CRUNCH! The sad news breaks
That clever boys can make mistakes.

Max Fatchen

The Computer's First
Christmas Card

jollymerry
hollyberry
jollyberry
merryholly
happyjolly
jollyjelly
jellybelly
bellymerry
hollyheppy
jollyMolly
marryJerry
merryHarry
hoppyBarry
heppyJarry
boppyheppy
berryjorry
jorryjolly
moppyjelly
Mollymerry
Jerryjolly
bellyboppy
jorryhoppy
hollymoppy
Barrymerry
Jarryhappy
happyboppy
boppyjolly
jollymerry
merrymerry

merrymerry
merryChris
ammerryasa
Chrismerry
asMERRYCHR
YSANTHEMUM

Edwin Morgan

School Crime

'So you say your school's been burgled,'
the policeman scratched his face.
'And there's nothing left to write with . . .
. . . this looks like a pencil case!'

John Rice

It's Such a Shock

It's such a shock, I almost screech,
When I find a worm inside my peach!
But then, what really makes me blue,
Is to find a worm who's bit in two!

William Cole

'ware Tomato-Juice

An accident happened to my brother Jim
When somebody threw a tomato at him—
Tomatoes are juicy and don't hurt the skin,
But this one was specially packed in a tin.

Anon.

Bathtime

Bathtime   lark time
                            plastic shark time
                            . . . fish and mermaids
                            purple ducks.

Bathtime   laugh time
                            really daft time
                            screams and wiggles
                            coughs and spits.

Bathtime   bedtime
                            soon be mine time
                            when Dad's finished
                            I'll get in.

Peter Dixon

Bursting

We've laughed until my cheeks are tight.
We've laughed until my stomach's sore.
If only we could stop we might
Remember what we're laughing for.

Dorothy Aldis

Acknowledgements

We are grateful for permission to reproduce the following poems:

Gerard Benson: 'Lim' from *Evidence of Elephants* (Viking, 1995), copyright © Gerard Benson 1995, reprinted by permission of the author.

Anthony Browne: 'At My Birthday Party' first published as 'I had. . .' in *The Much Better Story Book* (Red Fox, 1992), reprinted by permission of the author.

Dave Calder: 'Comicosaurus', copyright © Dave Calder 2003, first published in this collection by permission of the author.

James Carter: 'What Makes Me Me', from *Cars, Stars, Electric Guitars*, copyright © James Carter 2002, reprinted by permission of Walker Books Ltd.

Charles Causley: 'Old Mrs Thing-um-e-bob' from *Collected Poems for Children* (Macmillan Children's Books, 1996), reprinted by permission of David Higham Associates.

Peter Dixon: 'Bathtime', from *The Colour of My Dreams* (Macmillan Children's Books, 2002), copyright © Peter Dixon 2002, reprinted by permission of the author.

Bill Dodds: 'Could Have Been Worse', copyright © Bill Dodds 1991, first published in *Kids Pick the Funniest Poems* edited by B. Lansky, (Meadowbrook Press, 1991), reprinted by permission of the author.

Richard Edwards: 'Oh, Ozzie!' from *The House that Caught a Cold* (Viking, 1991), and 'The Wizard Said' from *Whispers in the Wardrobe* (Lutterworth Press, 1987), reprinted by permission of the author.

Max Fatchen: 'Dinosaur Department' from *A Paddock of Poems* (Penguin/Omnibus, Australia, 1987), reprinted by permission of John Johnson (Authors' Agent) Ltd.

Douglas Florian: 'Something's There' from *Bing Bang Boing* (Harcourt, 1994), copyright © 1994 by Douglas Florian, reprinted by permission of Harcourt, Inc.

Harry Graham: 'Appreciation' from *When Grandmama Fell Off the Boat: The Best of Harry Graham* (Methuen, 1986), reprinted by permission of Laura Dance.

David L. Harrison: 'Elephant Rules' from *The Boy Who Counted Stars* (Wordsong, Boyds Mills Press, 1994), copyright © 1994 by David L. Harrison, reprinted by permission of the publishers.

Christopher Isherwood: 'The Common Cormorant', copyright © The Estate of Christopher Isherwood, reprinted by permission of Don Bachardy, Executor of the Estate of Christopher Isherwood.

Mike Jubb: 'Bare Back Riding' first published in *A Poetry Teacher's Toolkit* by Collette Drifte and Mike Jubb (David Fulton Publishers, 2002), reprinted by permission of the author.

Doug MacLeod: 'Kitty' from *The Fed Up Family Album* (1983), reprinted by permission of the publishers, Penguin Books Australia Ltd.

Roger McGough: 'The Cabbage is a Funny Veg' from *Sky in the Pie* (Viking Kestrel, 1983), copyright © Roger McGough 1983, reprinted by permission of PFD on behalf of Roger McGough.